POLE DANCING

IN THE NIGHT CLUB OF GOD

Walter Bargen

ISBN 978-1-952204-02-9

Printed in the United States of America

RED MOUNTAIN PRESS

Seattle, Washington

www.redmountainpress.us

Early Praise for POLE DANCING THE NIGHT CLUB OF GOD

Let me posit that poetry must first entertain, in order to enlighten. This prose poem collection, Pole Dancing in the Night Club of God, is Walter Bargen at his finest. True enough, but I would venture further to say it is contemporary poetry at its very best.

Here the poet describes the adventures and misadventures of Adam and Eve, Moses, Luke and Paul, The Carpenter et. al. as Everyman in a colloquial, modern day society. Bargen is a bottomless wellspring of lush, mind-boggling images that leap and bound throughout the collection. Each line is masterfully crafted; and not one click of the telegraph here—a surprise awaits each step.

Without the slightest concern for hyperbole, I say I've not been more entertained by a book of poems for years. The humor, and there is plenty, is hilarious, dead on, yet affable. I am reminded of the old saw: "If you want to hear God laugh—tell him your plans." At times, Pole Dancing in the Night Club of God is bathed in humanity; and at other points, bristling with it. Bargen is among the keenest observers of nature, two-legged and the rest, writing today. It is prescient of the times we are certain to come face to face with in our fast-approaching, discombobulated future.

I've heard it said the definition of spirituality is awareness. If so, this is a holy book.

—Robert Nazarene, founding editor, *The American Journal of Poetry*

Imagine you are on a highway somewhere in the Twilight Zone and have checked into the Bargen Apostolic Motel; that Moses, the night clerk, hands you the quill of a pigeon feather dipped in lemon juice, but when you sign the guest book your name doesn't show up; that Noah lives up the highway in a double-wide; that the Bible next to the lamp in your room was placed there by someone named Ozymandias; that before Eve, Adam had a quickie with someone named Kandy, as memorialized in a yellowed copy of Edith Hamilton's Mythology; that Matthew, Mark, Luke and John are kitchen appliances who have dinner parties with Moses and the water heater; that you can only get three channels on the TV: a religious network where an Art Fern-type prophet sells less and less and less of everything; a Sci-Fi network where Godzilla and Goliath contemplate returning to a Gomorrah overrun with an epidemic of "big-fat-feet;" while on the remaining channel a worn-out G.I. Joe complains about all the "extravagantly filmed deaths" in the war movies he hosts. This is just a taste of Walter Bargen's "Pole Dancing in the Night Club of God," the unnamed narrator contemplating his thumbs with "only a few days left." Yet, lest we think all is "Atomized," we find such lyricism as "…the sky shot through with clouds as if something vast is about to be spoken…" or "The click of arthritic branches are a thousand white-tipped canes feeling along the wind," or such sage observations as "Everyday the world ends and no one notices." Yes, we will stay here a night, two, listening to what's left of the wild as it "lumbers low along dark sidewalks dragging a heavy tail," in hopes the past doesn't come back "armed and shooting again." Bargen has pulled off a sly miracle of social commentary you won't be able to put down.

—Robert L. Dean, Jr., author of *The Aerialist Will Not Be Performing*

There is something very serious at work beneath the wit, irony, wordplay, juxtapositions of time and place, and flat-out roaring existential humor in Walter Bargen's new book of prose poems. A biblical cast of characters is at work and play in the contemporary world, and they stand in for all of us in their daily struggles and frustrations.

Bargen's choice of the prose poem fits his voice perfectly; there is a credibility to these reports and also nifty phrasing, fresh inventive lingo and imagery, and amazing specificity indicting the human condition and questioning any metaphysical underpinnings. This is modern man/woman at the end of their tether, informed by all that's come before and often failed. We can learn something here and enjoy it.

—Christopher Buckley, Editor of *Miramir* and author of *Agnostic: Poems*

POLE DANCING

IN THE NIGHT CLUB OF GOD

CONTENTS

Prologue

Thumbing Through the Book of Days

Take my thumbs for example: not overly long nor out of proportion
with the rest of my hand, though longer fingers might have helped,
if I'd ever followed through on racing up and down the neck of a guitar,
stretching for impossible chords, or the reaching down into a warm
moist cleft for that other music. They are pinkish, though more a light
blowing sand unless flushed with blood, but more likely on a cold day
carved a statuesque alabaster from poor circulation. Held next to each
other, not quite mirror images, fraternal not identical, their two quarter
moons nailed to prehensile tandem orbits, working together even when
unscrewing a tight jar lid, the torque in opposite directions. If thumbs up
is a little phallic, it can't be helped, they are only commiserating from
different sides of the same dismal dilemma. The scattered scuff of clouds
that drift slowly across their sickle moons toward the nail clippers,
bruises or seasonal vitamin deficiency, I don't know. The soft wrinkled
details of hairless cross-hatched skin along their length and the deeper
furrowed joint where motion is planted and replanted—so many details,
but not the fumbling moniker of "all thumbs," not the vulgar "sitting on
his thumbs," not the soccer stadium in Santiago, early 70's, after the
coup d'état, where thumbless meant the guitarist's hands butchered by
soldiers. Even Ozymandias could not find his thumbs in a vast sand sea,
and I have only a few days left.

BOOK I

ATOMIZED

His diagnosis not yet in, Adam has lost his Dog, still he grips the collar in his hand trying not to let go. Arm out-stretched, his body turned sideways, he's yanked along by what isn't there. He refuses not to see four long legs, floppy ears the length of shoe tongues, Groucho Marx eyebrows, a two-tone tail curved upward except when thunder belts the windows. He's doggedly tried not to lay blame but responsibility lies invisibly curled on the couch and cowers in a corner.

In the yard, Adam ties the collar around an oak trunk. He offers it an old soup bone. He listens to the tree bark. It howls its leaves into the sky. A hind leg of wind scratches vigorously. He walks in circles around the tree digging a rutted path until the webbing frays and the lead snaps. Then the tree runs off and his business is no longer circumference. Adam's left with the straight and narrow arrow of grief.

Soon he's collared the table. Tries to walk a chair but it keeps falling on the first step down the stairs. The lamp chases the tail of its own light knocking papers from the desk onto the floor. At the last, he waits by the door to be let out, pacing back and forth, a spiked collar around his neck, the leash in Eve's hands, determined not let him run off to the gods again.

Should have thrown it out years ago, Adam thinks. Bookshelves already crowded with rocks and postcards, bookmarks and travel kitsch, all that Eve threatens and does throw away when he's not around, on a trip, or beyond recall. Adam uncovers a 26th printing, last copyrighted 1942, Mentor paperback edition of Edith Hamilton's *Mythology*, darkly yellowed as if not read enough or read too much but not recently.

He notices in Hamilton's book another signature below the title, in larger letters and more graceful than the author's. On the blank page opposite the table of contents inscribed within the elegant curves of a penned heart, an overly fletched cartoon arrow pierces the upper right chamber, projecting out the lower left, and split apart by that bloodless shaft the names Kandy and Adam.

Kandy skipped inscribing the love stories of Cupid and Psyche, Orpheus and Eurydice, Pygmalion and Galatea. It's not until the last section title, as if she'd grown tired of waiting, that Norsemen is crossed out and replaced with The Mythology of Kandy. Genealogies furiously fell: The Principle Gods now The Principle Kandy, no longer Perseus but the Ancestors of Kandy and Hercules, Troy captured yet again but by the House of Kandy, even the Index is reindexed Kandy.

At work, he explains the company catalog, the pages an uncharted bureaucratic sea where Aegean serpents scroll the margins. Adam echoes what he knows about lead times, delayed delivery, the difficult swinging dock doors, distant cousins of Scylla and Charybdis. He's less sure of Kandy, whose spell lasted maybe three weeks forty-five years ago. Eve quick to discard the faintest myth.

This heat-wracked Gomorrah is suffering an epidemic. Big-fat-feet congestion is worse than rush hour traffic. One-way signs don't reduce the trampling. Homelessness, tent camps, cardboard shelters, all collateral damage before fat feet head for the exurbs.

The city council debates an ordinance outlawing feet too large to pedal bicycles. The jails are filled with ponderous, depressed, frying pan-sized, flat-footed feet. To make room drug dealers and users are given early release: Tukano Indians convicted of eating yage, Indo-Europeans for drinking amanita mushroom smoothies, Southwest Indians lost in peyote visions, all set free. At five o'clock in the afternoon the city comes to a stop, congested with hallucinations, fat feet, and quitting-time traffic.

Stores don't sell shoes large enough. Physicists are called in to recalibrate the gravitational pull as the earth is daily compacted by big fat feet. Sensitivity training is conducted by linguists and anthropologists. Restaurants are going broke posting "No shoes, no service." The tax base erodes. With no money for repairs, the sidewalks are spidered with cracks. Mothers all over the city are being rushed to hospitals with broken backs. Psychologists and concrete finishers are offering crack therapy. Godzilla threatens to return if these big fat feet don't get out and stay out. This is a one monster town. Goliath thinks otherwise as he rubs his blistered feet.

Adam and Eve are off searching for the Fountain of Youth and left their pets unattended. The neighbors are complaining again about one in particular and threaten to call the police. It's not that it hasn't tried, not that it hasn't taken their concerns into account, not that it hasn't kept the curtains drawn, waiting till evening strikes with its clouds of mosquitoes and claustrophobic humidity. This has to be a two-way street in this marshy suburb but that's not the way the neighborhood sees it.

If they just didn't look out their windows at night as it lumbers low along dark sidewalks dragging a heavy tail. It can't be helped when a stray dog comes barking, scaring the wits out of it and the scales off its back. Its bite is worse than its bark with a mouthful of bacteria that will bring down a horse in a couple of days. Dogs go down like popcorn. Pets should be kept inside. Is that too much to ask? After all, neighbors are violating the leash laws.   Is anyone born wild anymore? Adam and Eve scheduled to return from Eden next week.

Not an ounce of air in the hip's calcium outriggers: dense with marrow and tides of blood. Two featherless legs: thick-thighed, heavy-calved, over-boned knees, broad flat feet, clawless quarter-mooned nails—to perch and sleep on a windowsill out of the question.

Two arms and a fervid desire to rise, to alight on the eighty-eighth floor, if only for a smokeless breath, a respite from the sudden fermentation of fuel and the zealotry of heat. The bubbling steel of Dante's innermost circle.

Nothing that resembles quill, vane, barb, barbule, barbicel, hamulus, all that's needed to flutter to the eighty-ninth, ninetieth floors, and out over the river crowded with clouds. Perhaps a few feathery steps, a jump into the fire of flight where suit and blouse become billowing plumage, arms beating the air, feathered by falling floors.

One more deep breath, then the release, Adam can feel the annoying pain in his neck subside, his shoulders relax, his eyelids collapse into the tired wallows where he sleepily rolls after an hour of galloping from page to page. He's sitting at his desk dressed in a buffalo robe, a heavy shaggy pelt that he inherited from some near-nameless Wild-West relative. He's worn it for years in that transition between autumn and winter when he wants to delay gathering kindling to start a fire in the circle of stones on the floor in his high-shelved library room.

He feels a movement in the robe. Maybe even hears a faint rumble. At first, he believes it's Eve reaching under the fur for his naked body, but that's wishful thinking. Then he thinks it's the chair creaking as he continues reading. He jumps up as a faint cloud of dust begins to rise over his chest and the rumble turns to thunder, and he's certain it's not the ketchup-drowned hash browns from breakfast, but a hoofed indigestion galloping over his belly. He flings the sash open and throws the robe out the window. Before it hits the ground twenty grunting buffalo race out, stop their tonnage before reaching the street, and begin to graze his yard. His neighbors, raking and bagging leaves, have all run into their houses. At the window, naked, panting, wild-eyed, he nearly died in the stampede.

Adam's singing from the bottom of a brass bowl hammered from rifle cartridges. He reloads his voice and takes aim. No one is certain of the target. Some say heaven. Some say hell. Some say he's walking through the swinging doors that lead to 47 miles of barbed wire and not just the mall where all the shoppers spill their bags ducking for cover when his song shoots out of the hall speakers to reach number one on the charts. Centuries of theological disputation tarnish the brass.

When the chairs are thrown on stage the band doesn't stop playing. The bass and lead guitars welcome the audience's generous offer with a thank you and sit down to the endless chord progressions that lead them into the next life. Adam stands, his lungs a fully exposed page from Gray's Anatomy. The bars of his ribs are all that keeps him from exploding on stage. In the ceiling fan, a heart-shaped helium balloon rips apart its letters of L-O-V-E.

No one mentions the rising water. The music too loud for that kind of warning. Forever blowing bubbles is about to become a theme song. Guitars turn into paddles. The bass drum holds three men in a tub. Rub-a-dub-dub, the sea chantey heard all the way down to the end of the bar. The brass bowl caught by the current snags on a half-submerged tractor tire and sinks.

No squish, squish, Adam's feet are dry. Not even muddy footprints following his too predictable path. Nothing dripping off his shoulders, no hair matted against his scalp, as if he'd just stepped from the shower, or tripped and fallen into a kiddy pool, as he's claimed on other days walking past the front desk. So why this morning does Eve, the receptionist, mention that a Federal levee in Winfield a hundred miles away along the Mississippi is breeched? Adam stares at her between the closing elevator doors. Eve's cheeks puff out. She so looks like a poisonous blow fish that the Japanese eat as haute cuisine, hoping for only numb lips and not Davy Jones' locker.

A Chinese carp jumps through the closing elevator doors. A twenty pounder, the kind that knock people out of their speeding john boats unless they tie themselves to their seats, that bust noses and front teeth, that leave boats churning in mad circles, the beered-up captains unconscious. It slapped on the floor at his feet. Adam pushed the buttons to reopen the doors, but he was already deep into the second floor. Too late to throw Eve a lifeline or share a last breath.

Lunch: sitting at his desk, half listening to the radio, half eating, half reading something that demands more attention than Adam gives it, half-glancing at the computer screen, vaguely waiting for three halves to become a whole. Adam recalls a photograph of a reclining bronze and gold-leafed bull, canopied in the center of an ornate temple complex in Hyderabad. Marco Polo may have visited this place nearly eight hundred years ago and watched a similar ceremony. Eve, a Hindu priestess, stands on scaffolding that raises her to the height of the bull's head, two stories above the foot-beaten bare earth. She leans over and pours curried milk, a color halfway between lavender and magenta. Bucketfuls are splashed onto the bull's back. Its eyes cry milk. Its nostrils pool milk. Its lips run rivulets. Its neck wreathed in milk the color of a God's blood. In the lunch heat of South India, Adam's dizzy with the curdling heat that drenches Eve's soirée.

The heat will only get worse. Once there were twenty-plus species of honey creepers on the islands of Hawaii. Now there are thirteen species left and one of those is represented by three individuals—all but extinct. Sure there are causes, and Adam could blame the victims for their own extinction: too highly specialized to a too suddenly changing environment with snakes, rodents, goats, and whatever else followed shipwrecks to shore. Then there is the pig gone wild that grubs the tropical forest floor, eats all the ferns, leaving a potholed landscape filling with rain that breeds pools of mosquitoes: malaria and West Nile virus abound. The surviving honey creepers with their gaudy splashes of green and lavender feathers, and their lovely, outlandish curved bills survive above six thousand feet these days where the temperature falls below fifty-six degrees Fahrenheit and the malaria bacteria doesn't survive. But each year the earth grows warmer and the honey creeper must move higher into the mountains that go no higher and, therefore, farther away from Adam and the sadness of curried sunsets outside his office window.

The book Eve has in her lap, that she moves to the desk, that the cat insists upon following and butting gently with its head, enough to make the words sway, fragment, and fall beyond reading, this series of scribbled glyphs cannot possibly say anything to this gray tabby, other than attend to me, attend the softness of my fur, stroke my purring with another slow hand down my back, rub just above my eyebrows, don't forget to slowly work the edges of my ears between the pads of your thumb and index finger. This is the story the cat wants to hear, as it drools with pleasure and a drop of saliva falls onto the top of a page, puckering a widening circle as it is absorbed, leaving the slightest stain, residue of a virulent fluid that once infected Eve when it savaged her hand, once when it was wild and soon after it had been trapped, a saliva that contains bacteria found in the mouths of Komodo dragons, who bite their prey and then lumber after them for four days until they are too weak from infection to resist being eaten. And now this furry little dragon wants little to do with its old life, though it sits staring out the window with a longing that she understands as she runs her fingers through its soft coat, pick-pocketing affection.

Perhaps this book will survive the both of them, paper tougher than flesh, though the book is helpless to ward off the infections of dust and mildew, what any secluded room has to offer before the quaking and flooding, fires and assorted conflagrations, or more simply the move to discard, that these words were at most an entertainment, a dalliance, a tale, an allegory to keep the mind turning through time, to unsettle the dust, but a hundred years from now, if there are readers who know, who remembers this language, if they should randomly turn the page and see this faint circle of wavy paper where a cat once happily lolled and expressed itself, what will they think, that a century past someone held a nightcap, a bourbon and water on a humid night, the glass streaked with condensation and confession, and balanced over this page, dripped, that this was one way to get through to morning, or might the readers see a moment of overwhelming grief, mainlining some loss rekindled by these lines, or would a cat be considered that affectionately drooled once one afternoon upon this page?

Forget the fig leaf, Eve really hasn't tried anything on yet, and probably won't, but she's shopping around for the right disease. At first she thought the more exotic the better though exotic has its own limitations. Geographically speaking, the common cold could be exotic in Antarctica. Ebola more than exotic where she lives but uncommon is probably not a good candidate either. Malaria with its uncertain outcome, perhaps years of flash fevers and night sweats, not certain enough. Hemorrhagic fever more certain but more random and difficult to find. And there's no control over an aneurism. Who can say when the heart will explode? Perhaps she will have to settle on an industrial grade cancer. But really, it's all the same or, at least, it ends the same, and so she takes another bite of the apple.

Adam and Eve sit across from each other, arguing all night: her
sensations versus his rationality, her Spinoza against his Hume. They
laugh at Descartes in the next rickety wooden booth, as he undresses
himself, searching for something certain and absolute. He's already down
to his holey t-shirt, as he worries over the "persistent vapors of
melancholy."

Down into their empty glasses, no Taoist half-full-half-empty-middle-way,
they're beyond that by years. Ralph Einstein walks into the bar,
unleashing his frazzled mop from under a red doo rag, buys a round for
the house, declares a toast to time, declares their worth is all in the
passing—curved space, warped lives, all that they can see in this stale
smoky strobing jukebox light.

Adam begins fishing for pocket change, making lewd jokes about
grounding their knowing as coins spill to the floor. Quarters flash across
the table. They head for song-machine salvation in a sequin-studded,
hip-thrusting Elvis tune. Across the dance floor they sweat beer into
each other's arms. Naked Descartes shouts, "I'm surprised by how
prone my mind is to error!" as Elvis swallows another note from a
heartbreaking universe.

Book 2

MOSAIC

Maybe Moses writes the note just to see if he can do it, to see if he has anything to say. Maybe he thinks it's just too good to be true. Maybe he wants his own secret, one that God won't know about. Maybe he just doesn't want to share everything, especially after the stone tablets. Maybe he doesn't know if he knows enough to really have a secret. But if he wants to share, all he needs is a candle and a match.

He does a test, squeezing juice out the cut-in-half lemon, dips the quill of a pigeon feather he found in an alley, and writes something, a few words of encouragement or disdain all directed toward himself, then strikes the match with its literary glow, holds it under the piece of scrap paper until the juice begins to brown as if some small passion is writing the words. He is no longer responsible and can blame the match for all the banality until the paper catches fire and momentarily rises into the air, a brief black flight of notoriety before falling in ashes. Now he can write invisible messages to no one in particular.

Maybe that's something of what McArthur Wheeler, 45 years old, had in mind, all 5 feet 6 inches, 270 pounds of him, when he entered Fidelity Savings in Brighton Heights and Mellon Bank in Swissvale, and the bank on South Fairmount starting at 12:10 pm, on a cloudless sunny day, gun pointed and no disguise, no Groucho Marx mustache or Joker mask, no white beard, robe, and staff. He was clearly visible to the surveillance cameras, and all he could say after arrest was, "But I wore the juice."

Under interrogation, McArthur claimed to have run a test in front of a
bathroom mirror. The lemon juice burned his skin and his eyes, forcing
him to squint. He even snapped a Polaroid and he was nowhere in the
picture. Perhaps the film was squinting too hard or out of date, perhaps
the camera was faulty, perhaps he pointed the lens in the wrong
direction. True or not, the gravity of belief is what holds the universe
down for another day or two, so Moses continues with his lemon juice
memoirs; it's what comes over him sometimes, writing the unreadable.

Heat and a junkyard of weeds crashes down around her. Humidity rises in clouds, as she swears deeper into earth's intimacy. Zipporah's lost in the garden, heaping the wheelbarrow with the skeletons of last year's growth. With clippers she trims the shaggy grass around the hydrant. She hauls tomato stakes wreathed in rags from where they huddle against the fence like tattered antique men debating prophecy. She can't outrace the sweat that melts her blouse to her body. She dissolves into salty earth before Moses notices.

Zipporah can't stand to be inside the house. Moses stands watching from the glass cage of a window as if he's still pole dancing in the night club of God. He wants to reach out, but the panes won't part. His instructions are to turn down the water heater's thermostat, clean litter boxes, vacuum upstairs, and not until it is done can the rain start, at least, that's what Moses thinks, but his neighbor, Noah, living in the double-wide up the road has a different water project in mind.

Of course, Moses has second thoughts, self-recrimination is a little too easy, easing him into the hard landing of denial, but there it is in the barn as if it belonged there, had always been there, an eternal chrome presence. But what was it, wrapped in scintillating ribbons of light that blow in through cracks between the barn's weathered gray siding? The sun dances through and applauds every newly exposed angle of his excitement, his passion for pole dancing.

Maybe it's similar to the spiral staircase in the tick-infested back forty beside the pond that's nearly dried up after years of drought, an empty mud-cracked socket of a blind eye. People keep showing up to mount the stairs, where Moses goes to pick up their abandoned Gucci, Prada, Rolexes, and Versace to fill the shelves of his secondhand store, Desert Rags, midway down Jerusalem Avenue on the southwest corner of Oasis Street where the sand dunes are over-parked. He wonders where the people have gone and worries if they might return to collect their abandoned possessions.

He pushes the straw far enough away, so his feet are clear to move. His hands brush only the manure-stained soil of the barn where he bends to raise his feet above his head. He air walks toward his own cloud pumped out from the dry ice machine. He's changed from his Carhartt overalls into black patent leather lace up boots with six inch chrome heels, a black leather corset to contrast with his celestial sparkling booty shorts, a thick layer of lipstick called Sin, and riding crop that he uses to whip himself up the pole as he reaches for a heaven that remains out of reach as he seductively slides down. Moses always slides back, and conceals his disappointment, his doubt, by circling the encircling of the pole with pirouettes that help him remember that he is just a part, a small arc of the circumference of circumstance and belief. His overabundant beard drips sweat. Creaky wooden stairs, chrome pole, it's all the same, working on this desire for transcendence, the Holsteins in their stanchions jostle, nervously waiting to be milked.

Wrenches working against each other, the pieces don't easily disassemble flat washers, lock washers, machine bolts, self-threading screws, all obstacles. This is a repair forced upon those wandering the desert of poverty. The housing around the rear wheel is a rusted through star chart. Moses glimpses God whispering in the buck brush amid the chiggers and ticks and ignores him as he works in the yard.

Out west, in Arizona and Colorado, fires are consuming hundreds of thousands of acres. Whole mountains of pine are pyramids of flame. Egyptians pharaohs would be envious. Night a transcendent glow. No face rising in a forest of flames, no scorched silhouette on a burned tortilla nailed to a restaurant door, no one staring down in a certain slant of light from a water tower. It's Sunday, Moses is busy converting his push mower into a self-propelled believer.

Moses returns home from work an hour early. He hangs his jacket in the hall. Forlorn piles of hats on the shelf above the coat hooks have lost their heads forever. He slowly changes into a dirty denim work shirt and jeans. A doomed prisoner, or just another hung-over day, he trudges toward the utility room. He doesn't bother with the light switch; instead he holds a flashlight. He observes each bolt spaced equally around the edge of the steel plate as they furtively weep warm water. There is so much to cry about. On his knees, he picks up the wet rag and wrenches. Moses never knew that a water heater could feel so much. Lonely and coated with dust, hoping to assuage its leaky feelings, he invites the water heater to dinner. The water heater accepts and asks if it can bring a couple of friends.

Around the heavy oak table, the water heaters listen to each other's stories: the yowling cat that was stuck between a forty gallon steel body and the concrete wall, watching the once-a-month affair between two plumbers making unnecessary repairs on each other, the circuit breaker with a short that sparks and sputters to the tune of Heartbreak Hotel. With the second bottle of Pinot Grigio emptied and the third just opened, the telephone starts ringing, the neighbors calling to ask: "Have you seen our water heaters? Downstairs there's nothing but gushing pipes!" Moses wades into the hot water again.

The room: one window east, one south, door to the north
opening on a short hallway that quickly turns to a stairwell that
descends to the basement. Ceiling, floor, closet, one can only
imagine the celebratory possibilities and know the story can't end
wandering across the bottom of a sea. It could be election night,
army of canvassers hoisting dozens of burning yard signs, suffering
a riot of belief on the street leading to where Moses is tied to
hallelujah. He doesn't bother with the ribbons and bows and looks
to Handel to lead the Que sera, sera, the What-is-to-Come
chorus.

In nowhere, out of nowhere, now here, now there, Moses stands insubstantial as shifting dunes. Hair on his arms upright, hair on his head pointing straight at the stars. A tremendous heat fuses him to the air: pillar of charcoal, pillar of ash, pilloried human in the square center of the round world. Dumbstruck. All he wanted was a name. All he gets is, I am what I am. Moses mumbles they are who they are, they went where they went. Bent over he empties sand fused into glass out of his sandals. Night-dazed, he carries half-a-rewrapped hoagie back to work on the graveyard shift, saving the leftovers for a promised land.

1

When one of his close friends died, Moses didn't attend the funeral.
Instead he read about it in the newspaper. It was next to stories about
extending the local hiking trail deeper into a wooded area where a
young boy disappeared, and a detailed schedule of performances, ballet
and string bands, for the upcoming downtown arts festival. The obit was
the usual puff piece, not that he would say anything bad about his friend,
but in a lifetime, there are always those troubling moments that are
ignored, glossed over, not mentioned. Moses knows there's no parting
from any of them.

2

He's at that age when too many of his friends have discovered their
ends, sudden and not so sudden. For comfort, Moses walks into the
kitchen. There's Luke the toaster waiting on the counter with a view of
the yard, there's Matthew the blender by the sink, there's Mark the food
processor, and John the can opener. They won't be found in any temple
orphanage or the manicured cemetery unless you think the summer
heat is toasting headstones the size of refrigerators, or in the clutter of
shelves in flea markets, waiting for the rest of the lost tribe to be
recovered.

At winter's end the lake loses its white wings and grows black legs.
Moses turns his back as the lake runs for its life toward the river. His
boots are sloshing through melting ice as morning strikes up its heat.

He's chasing a lake as he sinks into wet sky. Soon he flaps his arms as his
reflection brushes the tops of pines. He crawls through a quaking bog,
wallows in moss and lichen.

He's forming and reforming: gilled, scaled, a primordial descent. Moses
gathers and scatters. He fins chance currents hurtling between
mutations while asking for a refill at the local diner.

Water spurts a foot-high between the shifting ice pack, surges in small waves on the inlet's stone-strewn shore. This is as far as Moses will go, his decision chiseled across his face in cold and exhaustion. His cheeks blackened by dirt and the onset of frostbite. He's wandered beyond his desert. He's on his knees, not bothering, not daring to look out toward the frozen horizon. Tired of pointless gestures, he tosses himself forward then rolls over, not quite ready to enlist in the gathered flotsam of the beach. He pulls off a glove with his teeth, his fingers white, almost translucent, blood having abandoned his extremities. They belong to someone else's statue of praying hands.

The bus stops in front of the corner drugstore. Kids delivered from school crowd the entrance, not ready to head home or to hide in the park for a hand job or slip into the alley to stoke a joint. Moses can't hear a word they are saying. He's looking through them and the graffitied brick wall that rises behind them. Actually, he's not seeing anything at all, he's snow blind after days of crossing tundra, hoping that the next rise reveals something more than another vast frigid expanse of fatal cold light. He's floating on the darkness of the beach, when the bus diesels, lurches forward, jumps the curb and comes close to running down an aging derelict.

What was it he wanted to say to those kids strutting their stuff like goats, like dogs, the whole barnyard in heat, now that he sees them climbing out of a snow drift.. Moses can't formulate the first word as the yellow

bus opens its doors to let another passenger step up to a destination.
He's lying still, hardly aware that the bus has driven off on slabs of
floating concrete. Matching gloves his last thought before parting the ice.

Finally, ready to retire from the tribal business after all these years. For centuries, Moses chained to this or that leg of a sand dune, haunted by the worn-out joke of searching the desert forty years for a quarter. He packed light. He'd left the stone tablets in someone else's hands and they were quickly lost in a two-bit despotic desert honky-tonk. His favorite memento, the hoof of the golden calf, was bet and lost by a nephew in a Dead Sea casino. He did want to take his staff, but it was confiscated at the airport by a TSA screener.

He's flying to Utah. Plans to live rent-free in Moab at a friend's house who is gone most of the year, chasing the sun like a pharaoh in a fifty-six-foot-long RV. Surrounded by slick rock and snowcapped mountains, he wants the peace and quiet in order to complete his lemon-juice memoirs, something God will never read, but his cell phone won't stop ringing. It's the tribal accountant and too soon he's buried in millennia of unpaid bills.

Book 3

Damascus Rabbit Hole

Saintly

After a week of impenetrable fog, and unable to drive to the grocery store, it's served for dinner. The cook leans out the window and ladles three pots full. Cooked down and caramelized, it can obscure the most intense stare, exacerbate cataracts, even blind hatred. Fog-heaped steaming platters and no one knows who's sitting across the table much less whose elbow bumped the spoon, catapulting it into the air. All the guests sit mutely, listening for the metallic clatter of a landing but nothing echoes back from oblivion: no squealing like a stuck pig, no howling chains of a rattling coon dog, no caterwauling cat, no speeding tires chewing up gravel, no saw-scream of trees being subdivided, no sputtering machinations. Now someone will have to make do and wade in with a dessert fork.

Knives dance across the plates challenging the porcelain. There's never been a lighter cuisine except when saints lived only on light. No need to buy X-ray glasses advertised in the back of Marvel comics where the hair on the kid's head stands straight up in amazement, wearing oversized black frames with the lens spinning in mad spirals as a well-endowed woman walks past offering genius grants and foundation support. These superhero powers so out of control. The diners transformed from an accumulation of micro-droplets to photons. Now everyone can see through, stepping out of fog into the light. The road no longer needed, walking on air and water the rage as shreds of fog blow here and there. The long or short of it, Paul, the host, wishes the diners well, hoping they find Damascus one way or another while he purges their fog with a farewell Heimlich.

Paul thinks that he is suspended on air, but then it's rougher than the ungraded gravel that once found his house in the cedar woods. Or it's a deeper road, the road in the road that holds every destination that's ever been dreamed but now he's stumbling along covered in an asphalt nightmare. Or it's the road under the road, embryonic, not yet fully developed, certainly not ready for the likes of him, and if he drives on it too long all hell breaks loose. And maybe it's all three at once, as he begins to separate, turn into triplets, and watches himself watch himself headed in three different directions while claiming total control.

The steering wheel wants to set its own course, turning right, turning left, trying to center on three roads or no road at all as Paul begins to cry for the median. He was sure that he had a destination, but now he's not even sure that he was on a road that led somewhere, yet he's committed, no turning back, and hell bent to get there. He knows slowing down is a mistake, he'll end up dead in his tire tracks. There's no starting up again, tires uselessly spinning for years, a crazed potter's wheel. The thrown vessel looking like an unwashed car with tarnished change in the ashtray, the glove-compartment owner's manual and emergency flares about to ignite into panic. All three directions, all three lives, about to collide, and it's too late, the car's in mud up to its axles. Paul's heard Midwest farmers call this, "When the bottom falls out of the road," and he's driving on nothing to nowhere.

1

The long and winding road and they're only lost in northern Arkansas. A
Beatles CD blasts in the cab at two in the morning. Under flashlight and
a waning moon, the map says they're headed west when they needed to
head east to get to the Mississippi floodplain. Thirty miles back is the
missed turn. Should they keep going, leave the trailer, overloaded with
battered concrete forms for walling up dust and space, abandon them
on the shoulder of the road?

2

The road goes on forever. Mary's heard that before. At least, once with
each marriage vow, and now each time the Allman Brothers is cranked
higher on the CD player. The wailing nearly sends them careening off
the curve, as she plays lead guitar on the steering wheel. Forever, what
a crock, she thinks, a warning preceded by an expletive, seeing who's
sitting next to her: good, bad, and ugly all in one body. Following a
falling star, always a midnight wrong turn.

3

Yeah, one for the road, and one more for my baby, and another, and
another, but who could have guessed the road was twisted as Highway
1 following the coast along Big Sur. In San Francisco, the Sinatra choir
sings and swerves, swerves and sings. Mary wonders if any of the
barracks in the Presidio are child proof.

The phone starts ringing and Joe doesn't answer. He knows exactly where it's located on the heel-scarred, hookah-stained coffee table in the living room in front of the couch. He knows who it is and who it will always be, each ring grows heavier, as if resting on his chest, turning each breath into a labor of regret and paralysis. It's the phone call that keeps coming back from that day years ago when he was at the Bethlehem Fertility Clinic & Tattoo Shop that shared a waiting room, a dozen half-broken chairs, and a single receptionist. It's located on one of those beat-down dumpster side streets off Wilshire Boulevard, too far back to a have a view of a single gangly palm tree, but with its own permanent thermal-inversion ozone-haze.

Legs crossed and slouching so low he's sliding over the edge of the seat for a burial in a sea of chipped linoleum tiles as he day-dreamed a skull-headed butterfly with a lasciviously long uncoiling red proboscis that would glow under black lights in his bedroom. But first he needed to make a down payment at the fertility clinic in order to pay for the tattoo.

She sat next to him without saying a word. He could see it in her eyes. He no longer had the patience to read the waiting room magazines flaunting their headlines: First Cell Phone Pictures from Heaven, Freak Cyclops Born with Two Eyes, Judge Approves Keying Illegally Parked Chariots, Man Swallows Live Rattle Snakes. Without another word, there hadn't been a first one, they stood up, arm-in-arm around each other's waists, walked toward the door where a shriveled tortilla was nailed with the image of a skillet-scorched bearded face that he thought he recognized, but before they stepped over the threshold, the receptionist called his name for the Fertility Clinic. Mary followed him into the room and that's how he knows that he is the father and hence the damn angels keep calling to offer hush money.

The top half of the keyboard suffers a stroke, capitalization erratic, the shift key in need of rehab. What's on the screen could have been written by someone flunking freshman English. Holy is capitalized but not toledo. Batman is left nebbish and short-tempered all day. None of the numbers work either so he types the words for one hundred, not that Luke cares all that much, there's not enough left in the celestial accounts to steal. After his steep losses, the bankers and moneylenders are sunning their naked flab on the beaches of Trinidad & Tobago. All of these heartbreaking problems, but the lower case "i" still works, which must say something about the will to survive, to transcend, like the fabled cockroach crawling out of the refrigerator after a nuclear war.

Why does Luke care about Toledo and not Holy? The other day at work he walked both sides of the hall quizzing his geek coworkers on the subject. The next day he visited two high school art classes with a painting of a ragged black line against a darker reddish background. He suggested the silhouette was Don Quixote whose rusty armor was hammered by metal artisans in the city of Toledo. When asked what country he was referring to, no one in the class knew. He asked if they knew of any other place where there is a city named Toledo. No one knew. Returning to the office, two coworkers had never heard of Toledo, Spain, that place Cervantes described as a "rocky gravity, glory of Spain, and light of her cities," or of a Toledo, Ohio, immortalized in a song by John Denver, "they've got excitement to dazzle your eyes./You can go to the bakery and watch the buns rise."

Then there's Toledo, Iowa, hometown to George Struble, speaker of the Iowa House from 1881 to 1883 and an ardent prohibitionist. Toledo, Washington, first named Plomondon's Landing, then Cowlitz Landing, and later Warbassport. There's the Toledo settlement in Belize that was started by refugees escaping the U.S. Civil War, mostly Quakers and Mennonites. And Toledo, Brazil, in the western region of Parana, founded in 1946, where the annual Fiesta Nacional do Porco No Rolete takes place, where no pig larger than forty pounds is roasted. Luke faces so many Toledo's and so little time on this holy flat earth.

"Tell me," the queen resumed, "are you of royal blood?"
"Better than that, ma'am," said Dorothy, "I came from Kansas."

Retreads rip open, long steel trailers groan, air suspensions hiss as trucks
crawl across prairie overloaded with night. At border weigh stations
bleary-eyed drivers step down, their cabs drowning in all night radio talk
shows that cry the Lord and welfare. Scales slip into sleep, the eclipsing
loads pass unnoticed.

Dawn, a smear of gray light. Fugitive cottonwoods crowd the eroded
gullies paralleling the road near Oakley and Quinter, names wedged
between uninterrupted walls of horizon. At Fort Hays sheets of wheat
cover backyards. In Gorham a young boy steps off the bus and the
diesel whine trails off with a coyote's high-pitched scriptures.

In Russell the irrigation pipes spill ancient rains on parched ground—the
Oglalla aquifer a diminishing prayer. Outside town arthritic derricks
pound their arms against plowed earth and empty sky begging for oily
prophecies. By the dumpster behind the used car lot, a rusty flathead
engine rests, remnant of lonely rides across plains to Junction City and
Jericho.

Wind scorches a billboard. Outside Manhattan a broken-windowed
church, its steeple fallen from rot, is stuck in the ground. In downtown
Topeka, the buildings are the splintered brick stalks of a deranged

cornfield. Bridges stand half repaired. Midday the sidewalks are abandoned to the heat. Nothing moves except the bus as it leaves the station.

It's the old story, wrapping heathens in pox blankets. Each evening ghost ponies race from the hills to attack the white clapboard houses. Inside rooms, in front of televisions, the watchers call the moan wind and circle into themselves. At the park entrance empty beer cans, fired too quickly, surround two tired howitzers.

His daughter places three books: Sand County Almanac by Aldo
Leopold, High Lonesome by Louis L'Amour, and a Peterson's Field
Guide to North American Birds, along with a flashlight and drugstore
cheater glasses in the coffin either side of her father's head. Can a reader
go any deeper?

She inherited the bookstore. Each week for one hundred eighty minutes,
from one to four on Saturdays, exact as Bishop Ussher's date for
creation, customers can browse the shelves. On the other days, they see
the flutter of books with binoculars through the grimy storefront
window. The dust of Aramaic devolved into English.

During the late mid-Nineteenth Century, the deceased was often buried
with a sturdy piece of twine tied around a wrist that wound its way out
of the coffin up to the raw unsettled earth where it was attached to a
small bell hanging from a small shepherd's hook, fearing premature burial,
or if one simply changed his or her mind realizing there was one more
book that needed to be read. The bell's jingling to alert the grave diggers
to come running, or stumbling drunk, or passed out in their own face-
down buried alive lives, their resurrection in a drained bottle.

Last week three teenagers were arrested, vandalizing a nearly forgotten
cemetery held hostage by waist-high weeds in a field outside Judea, MO.
Convinced no one cared, or it wouldn't be noticed for months with all
traces of who, what, why gone. Not thinking at all, they dared each

other to defy the mortal odds. They pushed over another stone, another eroded obelisk, declaring a farther fateful fall to the already fallen, as they stood drunk on the immortality of youth. They'd not read the not so fine print chiseled on the lichen-stained stones.

Every day the world ends and no one notices this revelation. But a few

know the past just grew too large, too heavy, too awkward, too out of

place. It couldn't fit into the seat next to them, or they couldn't fold it

enough times to slip it into their purses, briefcases, lives. It couldn't be

shoved into the bathroom, the door locked, key tossed out the window,

or they just got tired of watching it recline on the couch, eating potato

chips, draining another can of sky blue mountains, as the world sinks

below the horizon, while demanding another bag of Doritos. Call it

night, set an alarm clock, but John is counting down.

John thinks someone would notice driving home from work that the

edge of the world was gone, that he or she is no longer driving to

anywhere in particular; Pittsburg, KS, and Pittsburgh, PA, one and the

same, balancing the cup of coffee while adjusting the rearview mirror

hoping to review all that just passed. The passing never pretty: dust

devils, floods, emptying bed pans, the road-kill removal crew heaving

another mangled carcass onto the truck bed. All that is passing at the

moment, turning up the IV drip when no one is watching, the crying for

a higher dose of morphine as fingers blacken, fingers intertwined, holding

on to the dark and trying to comfort whatever it is that is coming head

on, a runaway train with an engineer dead of a massive heart attack, eyes

wide open seeing nothing.

Not too much difference, as John discovers, when it's time for summing

the up and down of what is yet to be discovered and trampled by his horsemen—all there, all gone—under rocks in the creek where the crayfish scurry to hide from his apocalyptic pastime, and the mayfly larva fill blogs to disseminate the free flow of information as if that can save themselves from their one-day lives.

for DC

It's not so simple, it never is, but you're surprised as you walk through the lobby of faux everything, forced to stare close and hard to distinguish the real. Standing by the sliding glass doors, what is this eight-foot tall bear, brown, black, grizzly? There are so many ways to distort a no-relation-to-bear smiling snout, as it stands on its hind legs. Buckled around its bulbous waist a magnum-magnum six-shooter, close enough to its faux furry sexless crotch to be an Elizabethan codpiece with just a little of the handle sticking up, crying out to try me, or shouting a warning to the potential target as you drag your suitcase past. The choice to enter or turn back to jump into the fountain across the parking lot and hide behind a life-size bronze-colored plastic moose, as lead whistles over your head to the tune of "Home, Home On the Range" broadcast from speakers mounted on the canopy as the behemoth buffalo comes stampeding from the landscaping around back. The wooden bear depends on you, a subliminal conjoining of sex and violence, even with its paws folded over its chest, holding a ten-gallon hat.

You hardly stand a chance, the odds always stacked against the new hombre in town, saddle sore from a turbulent airline ride, and no dinner-plate-sized belt-buckle award awaiting you as you deplane. You are quickly distracted and lost following the "By the Lake" sign to the outdoor-indoor pool, its interior walls painted with scenes of pine hills stretching from corner to corner where a cartoon raccoon with ballooning thighs walks along one ridge, wearing a smirk. Not sure what it's saying with so many of its ring-tailed posse humped, unmoving, on the roads' real shoulders. Where is the brushstroke roadkill?

The heavy log beams supporting the roof over the too-blue chlorinated water have you believing that civilization won't collapse under snow, rain, or heat, but the beams are hollow plastic concealing the frail limits of steel and concrete. You don't dare care, a dumbfounded deer-in-the-headlights, when confronted with two doors, Doe and Buck. You really don't know which one you are, your confusion city deep. You cavort and commune with your long-forgotten antlered ancestors stroked on torch-flickered cave walls. It's hunting season, hesitation time enough to squeeze a trigger, so you hoof your way through the Buck's door before you check in.

Open suitcase, a tent in the soot-stained snow drift. Forever unlocked, but not broken. The key lost in some terminal or taxi along the way. Why worry, theft so common it's natural. So natural, everyone carries a handful of dirty snow in their left hand.

The thrill of stolen pleasures in dimly lit rooms, alleys, back streets. The city wet with melting. What was swept under empty beds, lonely desks, and shoved into closets, not so different.

Windows warped by thick ice. On one side, a wavy frozen landscape. On the other side, the face of a wavy frozen landscape. Under a snow of suitcases mice vacation, gnawing on a tired leather-bound black Book.

BOOK 4

UNDER THE BIG TOP

What busy weeks following years of Easters: Gene Autry records "Back in the Saddle Again," and the demented cowboy president rides inanimate in and out of office.

The first Laundromat opens in Fort Worth and property values skyrocket in Houston.

San Francisco quakes and Einstein is gravely questioned.

Paul Revere is down with saddle sores as digital waving Chinese arrive.

Darwin dies proving the survival of no one.

Jayne Mansfield loves mules, tractors, and posing nude.

It keeps happening, toads and fish raining down in the middle of deserts and falling on the clay tile roofs of small Italian towns.

The first human shot from a cannon is the first human and not the last to miss the target.

The first patented zipper pinches a thin-skinned lust and weeks of resurrections hardly get the job done.

Jacob's grandfather, who loved playing poker, won his German grandmother from her brother in one late night dark corner behind the beer barrels in a Mainz warehouse in 1894. Her last name was Grebb. Her grandson, Jacob, never liked her after she said to him, "Too soon alt, too late schmart.!" At least, they emigrated before there were any final solutions. Fifty years later he's selling his house in a Chicago suburb where the local weekly paper headlined, Snake Invasion, just another Biblical plague. Too much rain, forty days more or less, tipping the scales, keeping buyers away, but not the snakes curled in corners of the basement, waiting for the dove to return with an olive branch.

Jacob's reading a Catholic Supply website learning about Joseph, St. Joseph, husband of Mary, earthly Father of Jesus, the patron saint of married couples, families, carpenters, and workingmen. Italian and Poles said to be especially fond of St. Joseph for his special powers in real estate transactions, discovered by nuns who buried medallions with his likeness on property they hoped to acquire for convents. Later, the medallions were replaced with plastic statues and the focus changed from buying to selling. The statue is to be buried upside-down in the front yard with feet pointing to heaven. He doesn't know why, maybe it's to keep others digging in the dirt for golden idols. It may face toward the home or towards the street, if Jacob wants his neighbor's home to sell, the one with all the junked chariots sitting in the front yard. The statue's location can vary: near the "For Sale" sign, in a flower pot if you live in a condo, maybe on each side of the house if you're in a hurry.

Maybe even in pairs with each statue's head and feet pointed in opposite directions, to cover all the bases.

After the home is sold, the statues should be dug up, the dirt left in the robe's plastic folds, and given a place of honor in the new home. He's not thinking of purchasing another house or wife, one of each is enough, but the Home Sales Kit includes a 3.5-inch plastic statue and laminated prayer card that is to be spoken as St. Joseph is buried in the yard. The testimonial says he's helped thousands. But then there's also the St. Joseph Worker's Home Sales Kit and the book, St. Joseph, My Real Estate Agent with the gift-boxed Fontanini 4.5-inch resin St. Joseph statue and additional Home Sales Instructions. Which one to choose, Jacob isn't certain.

OK, this is all that I have left, but that's only because I've drawn some line somewhere, maybe even in the sand, maybe in the parking lot of the liquor store, but I'm standing on a sidewalk, holding this bushel basket of rotten apples, pulled from a grocery dumpster. Rotten means fermenting, abuzz in a cloud of bees and yellow jackets, so I set the basket down, and place a small cardboard sign on top that says FREE.

OK, so the only thing I have left is this cracked and heaved sidewalk, which I can't even lift a gray corner of to see what's burrowing and/or thinking underneath, probably something with too many legs that move wave-like and want nothing better than to crawl up my pant leg. So I'll just stand on this crumbling concrete, a good distance from the brewing apples, so I don't end up speaking a mouth-full of assorted stinging syllables, and only have to deal with what's crawling up my calves. Nobody wants an inert chunk of weathered gray matter unless there's a revolution to start or just to raise hell or is in need of a heavy thought.

OK, no bushel basket of apples, no sidewalk, so the only thing I have left is this loopy line of telephone poles, leaning this way and that, like an uncrossable log jam on the upper reaches of a polluted river or a giant's just-started game of pickup sticks. All these conversations that can never right themselves and drunk on destruction, sure to end up in arrest or divorce, unable to even finish a sentence before the handcuffs clamp closed or the gavel seals the deal on sprawling circumstances.

OK, no bushel basket of apples, no sidewalk, no telephone poles, just this long line of parallel-parked rundown cars, and at 6 a.m., I could set up steroid-sized for-sale signs at either end of this short street, and by 8 a.m. the street will be sold out, cleared and ready for a window-busting home-run baseball game, except for the one car that had its battery stolen last night, and it looks so lonely being used for third base, as the ball disappears through the window of the second-story apartment across the street, and the whole team runs to their rundown homes.

OK, no bushel basket of apples, no sidewalk, no telephone poles, no used car lot, all I have left are the manhole covers and sewer grates, which will require quick teamwork to pump so much iron into the trunk of the car with the missing battery. It's the beginning of a booming scrap-metal business, but they're welded closed and padlocked, as if this good idea has already worked for someone else who has quicker gray matter and not just concrete.

OK, no bushel basket of fermenting apples, no spider-cracked sidewalk, no catawampus telephone poles, no used car lot, no embryonic scrap-metal business, so this is all I have left, prophecies I've made, good and bad, though mostly bad, and the disastrously bad cost the most, and laughing at my expense is a real money loser. I'll throw in a few insights shattered quickly as a baseball through a picture window, leaving just about as many sharp shards as available wrists. Anyway, Vladimir Lenin said, capitalists will sell us the rope with which we will hang them.

OK, I'll sell you swinging-in-the-breeze, cheap.

Esther opens the door to her office and the phone is ringing. Later, she opens the door to her house and the phone is ringing. Each time she reads the caller ID, it's the same Unknown Number. Each time she doesn't answer she grows more agitated. She begins to worry—what is it she doesn't know about what she's avoiding. Avoidance festers deep on the shelves of a refrigerator not cleaned in a year.

First it's tennis elbow that shoots pain up into her left shoulder. Then there are random spots on her back that maniacally itch until her fingers drill to new oily deposits. The fillings in her teeth begin to pick up radio frequencies. When she opens her mouth, she's broadcasting talk show rants. She makes a doctor's appointment.

The doctor prescribes a mixture of willow bark, bat livers wrapped in frog skin, and wriggling lizard tails, dead one's won't work, and a daily tablespoon of Dead Sea salt.

Esther gets lost in the woods looking for drugs jettisoned by dealers on the lam. She meets a man in the deepest part of the forest who keeps her married for forty years. He turns her bones to brass and they begin to ring each time she complains.

Finally, she escapes and returns to her house that needs a new roof. She hears ringing coming from the water circling in the drain, from little mouse paws running along the water pipes in the walls, the ringing of cat claws racing to catch them. There's no way she can answer the backlog of ringing when the doorbell rings. Esther stands clapper-still under a brass sky.

San Juan Islands, WA

He carried it with him into the bay, perhaps into the sea, and it was
washed back into the bay, this Useless Bay for any hull with a deeper
draft than a corked bottle holding only the message of a last breath.

A sliver of rectangular plastic tangled in kelp where the tide pulled back a
depth of six feet and the tidal flat stretched for a glistening mile. Faded
and warped from the pummeling of salt water, sand, and mud.

Perhaps already permanently below the waves, floating in another world,
his shoulder length dark hair fingered by the currents, nibbled by fish,
mimicking the undulations of prophecies, when he let go of his official
photo in the upper right hand corner, or nothing so final, just horsing
around in the water beside the boat and lunging up over the gunwale his
license fell back for a deeper drive, a languid seesawing to the bottom,
not realizing that his body would go unidentified except by friends, who
bear their own crosses.

If his photograph says anything, it's that he leads with an ear to ear smile,
solid as Mt. Ararat, and so explains why like any stone the bottom is a
good resting place. Some details are clear: 6 feet 1 inch tall, 160 pounds,
male, all of which point to a slender presence, and would add to
apocalyptic conclusions of the reed that bent too far back into the sea.
Licensed limitation, corrective lenses, plus an anatomical donor, though
which, when, and what parts are not specified for a shared immortality,
a kind of lateral pass to another body.

The repeated roller-coaster loops of the signature, as if the ride never ends, and at the date of issue he was thirty years-old and at thirty it doesn't until it does, and his parents know that, though uncertain which island would hold him longest. They wait, as all parents do, for their child to return from a long drive under the sea.

JERICHO'S COLD HORN

Under the Pole is the place of greatest dignitie.

—John Davies, 1595

A savage youth—though not clothed in beastes skin or eating raw flesh,
as John Cabot observed hauling back three Eskimos to die in King Henry
VII's court. A prodigal son who took his insurance settlement from a Las
Vegas car crash, not bothering with plastic surgery for the scar plowed
across his forehead, just another wrinkle in time, and the one carved
down his cheek, having dueled with death's chrome sword he was left
standing for a moment or two, and invested after losing most of it to the
slots, in a half- pound of magic mushrooms to take camping.

Half-a-day's drive south, half-a-day's hike, tents on a gravel bar by a small
river. Stone-ringed fire, flickering hub, Ezekiel's flaming-spokes wheeling
over driftwood ashes. A pine knot cornucopia, a wooden horn jazz-
lipped lasciviously, and laughter until he can't recall anything but laughter.

Through next morning's mesmerizing leftover hallucinations, he stumbles
upon a hermit's shack. A grizzled old man who first saw a silvered speck,
a plane over the valley, maybe early 1920's. Years later, the prodigal
son, now chemotherapy bald, his scars folded deeply into his red
wrinkles, says there was no hermit, that they entered the one room,
door hinged with leather straps, one wall lined with dusty novels, their
titles now forgotten. Always revisions to the living hallucination.

Outside the temperature has trouble counting up to zero: April 6, 1909.
Robert E. Peary lost nine toes just to stand at the Pole. By the kitchen

window crows gather in a bare oak. Cold slaps the house awake. At the table, he begins to sing. He's never done this before except to blow inarticulately a single note from a rotting pine knot. Surely there was a temple among those waist-high winter weeds.

The weather has stopped work for two weeks. Flurries throw a thin blanket over the already foot-deep snow. Day's dark stubble roughens his chin. Against the south wall scrubby juniper bushes are sheeted like white desks in a long-abandoned school. He's too old to be doing what he does, though he still feels the need to get out of the house, carry his sweat-stained leather tool belt to the truck parked in the driveway. His tools stored in a padlocked metal box bolted to the truck. Shovels and picks frozen to the rusting bed. His diploma hangs in the dim light of the bathroom.

Each morning, his back hurts, but he wants it to hurt more as he imagines bending over to pick up a stack of 2 x 4's or a sheet of plywood. The house a paragraph: studs and beams, subfloor and oak planks, windows and doors, all dependent clauses that staples, glue, screws and nails punctuate. Without a tool in his hand, there is no meaning to measure, to saw, to hammer, to shape. Another couple of weeks and he can apply for unemployment. Standing at the window, he unwatches cardinals and jays crowd the bird feeder. He sees the black feather of a comma float to the ground, winged parentheses that deconstruct as a cat outlines its hunger. On these long days of short light, he parses the house down to minutes and epic sighs.

Morning on Mars

> . . . every intellectual labor is a peculiar degeneration . . .
>
> --Zbigniew Herbert

The mosquitoes are hanging around after a wet spring. West Nile and malaria ride the hot surf of global warming north. Today I sit behind floor to ceiling porch screens. It hasn't rained in over a month, and it's easy to wonder if this isn't a plague of drought-resistant mosquitoes whining for a personal invitation as they tease the screen for an opening into flesh.

The sky a permanent gray but the forecast is a slim chance of rain. This my excuse for sitting here. The air smells moist, womanish, with a scent of dust and desiccated weeds. I hallucinate the small slaps of droplets like polite applause for a mediocre performance. The sidewalk dries faster than the arriving rain. Oak leaves continue to curl and wilt. Hummingbirds in the middle of the yard chatter around the feeder, unperturbed by everything but each other. A friend calls convinced our troubles date back four millennia as recorded by fragments of four or five clay tablets.

Two giant brothers, Enlil, god of earth, and Enki, god of water, from a Sumerian myth—myth, my word not his. After a rebellion of lesser gods, fed up with the hard work imposed by the higher pantheon, the goddess Mani molds clay figures mixed with the flesh and blood of the slain god Geshtu-E . Are we mortal gods? After the god-spit-soaked clay simmers for ten months, black-headed slaves are born. Disillusioned,

disappointed, disgusted by people reproducing faster than rabbits or cats
and the rampant plagues, the two brothers decide to abandon this
backwater planet and destroy all the humans in a great flood, but
compassionate Enki gives plans for an ark to the hero Atra-hasis.

My friend says all our troubles date back to when we were created to
be slaves. We were infected with brain parasites so we're ready to
believe that nuclear power is clean energy, that these plants should be
built on the fault lines. He's sure the gods are seeking to close the dusty
account they left open millennia ago. What can I say, cats infect rat and
humans brains with toxoplasmosis, a parasite, that increases the chances
of depression, suicide, and an increased rate of male births among
infected women. Rats come to love cats until they are eaten. The
Egyptians knew who to worship, Bastet, the cat god. What more is
there, knowing we have more bacteria and viruses in our bodies than
human cells. Who is really riding the bus downtown? Maybe life on
earth is extraterrestrial, when a Martian mass was catapulted into space
during meteor impacts, careening down to impregnate earth. The human
virus now destroys earth with or without Enlil and Enki.

Where the Satan-worshipping families of Monaco fit into this I don't
know or that the Book of Mormon is really a Mayan codex that was
written on gold leaf and hidden from Cortez, rediscovered by Joseph
Smith, that aliens have trouble with earth's gravity and want to know
how we can stand to live here, which must be a joke he missed. At the
Cahokia Mounds, the earthen pyramids in the Mississippi River
bottoms east of St. Louis, dousers in 1948, the year of my birth and that
must have something to do with this message he is sharing, located

underneath the steep grassy slopes buried giants. Enlil and Enki?
We won't know till the government lets someone excavate. The
Martian mosquitoes continue to whine outside the porch screen with
the grief of many little bloody goodbyes.

--for DM

A wall of green has grown up around the house in another lost city. Seven-feet high wild lettuce stalks block the view from the kitchen window, as if the whole house is a tossed salad. Sunlight and a lattice of leaf shadows crisply crisscross the linoleum that's rolling in disembodied cat fur.

Leibnitz sits down for 4 to the 4th power days in a row to eat oatmeal with exactly 11 halved walnuts, 12 blueberries, and a single tablespoon of maple syrup, but not for long. First, he sneezes, then sneezes again. God has to work overtime with blessings. Then he gets up to pull a tissue from the box on the counter by the door to blow his nose, then a second.

He takes a sip of coffee hoping that it will settle him down. His sinuses are a welling up underground aquifer—the Ogallala has nothing on him. He reaches for another tissue. The early summer morning is densely humid. Pollen-spangled light streaks through the room. He reaches for a handkerchief and inhalant, God's calculus clouding the air.

BOOK 5

REVELATIONS

An afternoon of falling plaster, as if this were the weather forecast for the century; as if this were on the calendar and it is the name of a month like Moon of Popping Trees or Moon of Buffalo Breath, this the Moon of Falling Plaster. In the room, it's no good shielding his head, his arms would turn blue and numb if held up for that many years of afternoons.

Seen from a distance, someone might call the cops believing a robbery in progress. Someone else might call the bishop, believing a Druid ritual, sun worship, cloud worship, the angel of air bellying up all around, or worse, call for an exorcism, seeing satanic possession, as he claws the sky going to pieces above him.

Then again, there's always someone ready to commemorate a new park statue, his arms too willing to march off without him and embrace the eternal bronze of late afternoon. He has no thought to reclaim them, his white flag solid as Roman marble sunk in the Bay of Naples.

Why no one thought hands-over-his-head was not the perfect gesture of a century as he was marched across a field to an open ditch? No one to call back those ragged, trembling hands, no one to recall the explosion of plaster.

—for Kevin Walsh

EXILE

> The universe is a solitary place, and all its creatures do nothing
> but reinforce its solitude.
>
> —E.M. Ciorin

A young woman walks along the street listening to the creak of doors opening, so familiar, she gives them names, each baptized in this light morning rain. From the second floors of houses, the sibilant slide of sashes and the stale air of bedrooms rush past faces that surface from another night of drowning in feathers. Their heads flutter down into day's dull depths.

Each morning she walks a different street, listening to the arguments pick up where they were dropped the night before: on top of kitchen tables stacked with unpaid bills, in sinks clogged with scummy water, porches cluttered with recriminations, and nothing is allowed to be forgotten, nor to be covered by sheets and blankets, nor swept into the dust under the bed, each half-hung-over reason will do to strike out and add to the world's rubble.

Each morning she is on her own in this refugee choked city: cheek to jowl, cumin to curry, sweat to sweat, God against God. She is the girl whose parents were dragged from their house, stood in the glare of headlights, the backfire of a truck motor, and that's all she remembers. She can't speak their names.

Television belly up in the living room. The gray screen a puffy blank face. The unplugged gloom, once a fortune teller's crystal with color density dials and vertical control.

Radio on the table, the advertisements beat out of it. Everything else too: talk shows speechless, FM hosts mime how-to-lawn-care, dreaming grubs and crabgrass control, fertilizer application, flower bulb planting. The ground frozen to hell and back.

The refrigerator no longer hums a dull compressor tune. The nonchalant whistling of an ax with darkness to chop, silence to bludgeon, and little time to stack and burn the evidence. Circumstances to report: heavy clouds, horizons of glazed roofs, yards ankle deep in ice.

An aerial mausoleum surrounded by weather-beaten splintered oaks. Orders of exploded sky. Air masses on the march. What year of the war is this? Coffee rationed, sugar gone. Each minute reduced to a new craving.

Happy the people whose annals are blank in history books.

—Thomas Carlyle

Still wearing the many-pocketed, mottled camouflage vest over an army-green sweater from the most recent war, Tomaz stands at the base of the hill. Over his shoulder the sky shot through with clouds as if something vast is about to be spoken or explode against the blue-brass cartridge of understanding that might even be responsible for shaking the trees bare of their leaves on this bright autumn day.

Tomaz runs his hand along the edge of a sandstone block set on the back of a horse-drawn wagon. This his weighty proof, from three hundred fifty feet above a valley scarred with craters, covered with skull and cross-boned signs pointing at fields and the word mine in three languages, but no one making any claims to farmhouses that stare vacantly from busted windows.

On the summit of Pljesevica, this massive pyramid masquerades as a hill amid many hills masquerading as pyramids, all larger than those pin pricks at Giza, larger than the ornate complex of Teotihuacán, larger than the mole hills of Cahokia. Tomaz stands on his belief.

On the streets of Visoko, the ancient capitol, stores crowded with lucrative homages to a glorious past before the past comes back armed and shooting again. There are slotted clay pyramid banks for the day's small change, pyramid-engraved knick-knack boxes, pyramid-pointed leather slippers, and pizzas are no longer baked round.

Tomaz would found a country on upthrust sandstone stacked and cracked by tectonic plate-shifting, so wall-like, so cistern-like, so patio-flat, so that citizens of this small country can live geologically happy ever after.

Judas is tired of hearing about brave men, who only did their duty, the men who valiantly died, or survived with their wrinkled stories folded deeply in their pockets for sixty years and fill today's newspaper columns and TV screens on yet another anniversary of their disappearance.

The pilot who kept the shattered bomber aloft long enough for the crew to parachute, silk carnations blooming across a flak-festered sky, and then to crash in a field just beyond the small French village where the tall stem of a granite monument now stands. A tail gunner follows the smoke down each day of his wilting life and a president writes the screen play.

Judas is tired of extravagantly filmed deaths, men hired to act out heroics, the falling in slow and slower motion, the grace of time teased and stretched into last words and longer sighs. The audience last to get up, sweeping clean their popcorn-littered laps, heavy with sacrifice, wanting their own chance to charge the doors that open onto traffic-crowded, sunlit streets.

QUIXOTIC

Only the leaves tell the truth.

—Charles Simic

I

On a road he's never known, outside a city he'd forgotten, he opens his mouth to ask directions and all he hears is the windmill motion of a winded tree rising out of his mouth. Horseless, he is left with no way and no one to charge but himself. How long can this heartache last? One moment of pain is its own lifetime. Many moments of pain are many lifetimes, yet they coalesce into a man stumbling through a green haze, his only destination the tree he speaks.

2

It's the ash tree in the cave of his throat where the boar rubs, scratching its bristled back, where the hound bays, chasing the boar around the trunk, where the wolf watches, waiting for a mangled prophecy to drop as the tusked boar turns on the hound. Spectrums redden. One eye falls on the man, the other lost in the doorway of stars.

3

Only his body tells him that there is a left and a right, an up over his head, a down under his feet, his face caught between is headed in another direction. He meanders toward the tree blurred on the green-fogged horizon. Flocks of fireflies claim their stardom as stars flicker the celestial codes of fireflies. The cold tree looms high where a wolf's ebony howl is lodged with leafy stars.

93

4

The man is not afraid of losing his way. When he coughs he hears the rustle of leaves. When the sun finally rises, sadly, the wolves are gone. They are escaping that other universe where their kind are hunted from planes and poisoned by panjandrums. There is no Ariadne with a magnesium-white thread straight as a folded piece of paper to lead them on.

5

No sway-back bony horse headed through the valley of death, no rusty armor hammered by Toledo's blacksmiths or camo-Kevlar vest bought at a military surplus store, no trusty rotund sidekick to save his sorry self, just his dendritic desires within the unfurling root of his face, crying a primordial longing for that first moment, that first time, that split second before there was a first full second.

6

Time tickles the back of his throat. His blood begins to beat at the ashen doors of stars. Thousands of papery eyelids flutter in the branches of the tree. The reddening blush of autumn arrives, the leaves fall onto an exhausted star, the tree is left blind. The click of arthritic branches are a thousand white-tipped canes feeling along the wind.

7

The man knows how easy it is to lie down amid the raked piles of leaves, leaving his lance and armor to rust in the ripening of evening, in the soft sweetness of a decaying light. He can't delay the descent, can't stop the generous decline of flesh into flesh, which is only the beginning of another ascent into the vastness of stars. He doesn't know how it started even as he stands beside the road behind the white picket fence of his teeth.

ACKNOWLEDGEMENTS

With grateful acknowledgements to the editors of these magazines and anthologies where the following poems first appeared:

American Journal of Poetry — Global Warming on a Friday Night
God's Juice
Lost Music
Egyptian Pole Barn

Chariton Review — Ice Storm
Back from Extinction
Human Angels
Century of Testaments
Pandemonium
Morning on Mars
Buying the Commute
Checking In To Heaven
The So-Called Good Life
Exile
Post-Post

Classifieds: Anthology — Pyramid Scheme
Local Prophet Says Everything Must Go

The Freshwater Review — John's Baptismal License

Gingko Tree Review — Carp Before the Horse
Holidays
Apparellously Close

Helen Literary Magazine — Brain Storm

Midway Journal — The Great Flood Arrives Every Other Year

Moon City Review — Thumbing Through the Book of Days

Negative Capability — Collared

Prose-Poem Project — Curried Sadness
Evolution of Morning Coffee
Astronomical Allergies

Redaction — Eternal Appliances

2River — Saintly
Sigmund Road
Mowing
Stylish
Damascus, KS
Lost Music

Voice de la Luna — People of the Book
African Relatives of Komodo Dragon
Thriving in Florida

Quixotic was first published as a chapbook from El Grito del Lobo Press, 2014. Global Warming on a Friday Night was nominated for the Hanks Prize, 2018.

Many thanks to Matt Dube for reading an early version of this book, along with Zak Wardell, Lois Long, Sharon Singing Moon, Barbara Leonard, and Lynn Lampe who read many of these poems.

And very special thanks to Susan Gardner, founding editor of Red Mountain Press, for her keen eye and sound judgment in the editing and publishing of this book. Thank you.

This book is set in Gill Sans, designed by Eric Gill and based on the earlier 1916 font by Edward Johnston, the "Underground Alphabet", designed for the London Underground.